Chorali

By Roger Emerson

Pavane Cat #: P5033
Hal Leonard Cat #: 00466828
ISBN: 978-1-950736-05-8

Credits

Editors: Elyce Berrigan,
Andrea Fox
Sketches: Joshua Petker
Graphic Artist: Elsa Castañeda
Layout & Design: Allan Petker

Prologue

If truth be known, the most challenging part of this book was its title. Originally, it was simply "Things I Learned From The Choral Masters." I then added "and friends" as much of my philosophy has been distilled from close friends. Either way, it was deemed "too dry" by my publisher and others after reading its contents so…here are some others. You decide which one you like best…in fact, there is a place to write in your own title but you must read the book in its entirety first! How sneaky, Roger!!

"Sing, Dammit! Sing!" – my favorite, but deemed somewhat offensive ☺

"Sing Dagnabit! Sing!"- a bit less offensive

"Are You There Maestro? It's Me, Rog" – suggested by son, Ryder Emerson

"Wonderful, Raucous and Ridiculous Reflections" – clever but perhaps not reflective of the contents

"Amazing Amusing Asinine Anecdotes" – someone likes alliteration

"Amazing Amusing Musical Anecdotes" – someone still likes alliteration

"Sensational Short Stories" – I wish they were!

"Momentous Musings" – more alliteration

"Choralations Is Not a Word!" – getting close!

"Choral Quips" – not quite

And the winner is? *"Choralisms"* – Things I Learned from the Choral Masters…and friends ☺

According to the dictionary, an "ism" is a practice or process, a distinctive system or philosophy. That it is.

Your title? _____

(Think of something clever like: "Why did I spend $19.99 on this book!")

Any way you slice it, here's my book! It's the result of me keeping a manila folder with scraps of paper and Post-it™ notes for years to remind me of stories and events that have shaped my "choral" life. Some are funny and some touching but all are impactful.

I often wonder how I got so lucky that I get to make a living in music. It was never my goal, even though in hindsight, it seems inevitable as I was always surrounded by musicians, and the making of music pretty much consumed my childhood.

Nevertheless, I hope that you will enjoy the read and perhaps pick up a few pointers along the way. The chapters are short, often just a page. You will recognize many of the names, as they truly have been "choral masters" and have contributed greatly to our profession and my life.

In closing, I must share the kind words of my publisher and editor, Allan Petker, that I received after his first reading of my manuscript. It is perhaps the kindest, most validating note that I have ever received and I hope it informs your reading:

"Just finished reading through the book. Meaningful, rich, touching, useful. Wonderful! What a privilege to get to publish this thoughtful and intimate gathering of thoughts from your esteemed career." – Allan Petker

So, as they say in show business, "On with the show!"

"SYNCOPATION IS EMPHASIS ON A NOTE THAT IS NOT IN THE PIECE."

4th Grader

Part 1

The Masters

Howard Swan
"Dusty Pieces"

One of the best things about having your music published is that you get to interface with some of the best and brightest teachers and conductors and, believe me, I didn't take that bonus lightly. In fact, this book is filled with moments that have shaped my professional and, in some ways, even my personal life. Howard Swan is just one of those people.

Sometime in the early 1980s, I was asked to present a workshop in Minneapolis on popular choral music and the keynote speaker was Howard Swan. About eight of us were seated at the head table; we had just finished lunch and Howard rose and went to the podium. His voice was quite gravelly and rough as he had damaged vocal cords, if I recall, from an illness. In fact, he could not model for his singers and yet produced marvelous ensembles. Ponder that for a moment! He began his address with these words:

"Bach….Handel….Mozart…" (Then, turning to me) "…and even Emerson….have their 'dusty' pieces!"

I'm sure that I laughed along with everyone else, as in a weird way I was flattered that he had even included me in his keynote address, especially with the likes of those truly great composers.

He went on to talk about the pieces of each composer that have not seen the light of day and there is a reason…they're not very good. And, he's right! Some pieces are just better than others. Even though we...or I...make an effort to make every title excellent, some pieces just arrange better or are truly inspired. I have arranged or written more than 1,000 choral titles in the past 40 years, but I can count my favorites on my fingers and toes!

Having said that, I am reminded of a Q&A some years later when a student asked the question, "What was your least favorite arrangement?" It didn't take long to answer because I had just finished an arrangement that I did at the publisher's request called "Slow Down I'll Find You" from the latest Susan Anton movie. I did my best, but the song just wasn't very strong. To my surprise, a teacher in the back of the room began frantically waving her hands in the air. When I called on her, she said, "My kids just loved that song!" It just goes to show you that one person's coal is another's gold.

Howard's lesson? Just because someone famous wrote it, doesn't mean that it's good. Be discriminating. Use your musical sense. When I see an edition of a "masterwork" I'm not familiar with, I'm often not surprised that there is a reason it has not surfaced sooner...it's just not very good.

SIDEBAR: Howard Swan was Robert Shaw's first choral conductor at Pomona College.

Jester Hairston
"If Only I Could Arrange Like That!"

One of my earliest reading sessions (circa 1979) was for the ICDA (Iowa Choral Directors Association) held in Mason City, Iowa. For those old enough to remember, Mason City was the final concert for Richie Valens, Buddy Holly and The Big Bopper, as their plane crashed shortly after takeoff from nearby Clearlake. Don McLeann refers to that as "The Day the Music Died" in his hit song, "American Pie." I remember where I was that day in 1958....even at eight years old I was a big fan of pop music and "Donna" was one of my favorites.

I had just started publishing the year prior and had a very popular choral called "Sinner Man." I followed it with an arrangement of another spiritual entitled "Wade in the Water." As I prepared for my session, I noticed a familiar face in about the fifth row and to my right. It was Jester, his hands folded in front of him, smiling his toothy grin. I had met him briefly about 10 years prior when he guest-conducted a festival at College of the Siskiyous for my mentor, Kirby Shaw.

Needless to say, I was nervous. Not only was I conducting my own pieces, but they were drawn from the fabric of Jester's heritage and own success: African American spirituals.

After my session, he walked to the podium. I was expecting perhaps a "dressing down" as my treatments were set to a rock beat and quite contemporary in nature. I was relieved when he gave me a big hug and said, "If only I could arrange like that!"

On that day I learned a couple of things:
1. Don't pre-judge what you think someone else thinks of you and your work. You may very well be wrong.
2. Always be gracious. It goes a long way.

His validation, to this day, has made me a better composer and arranger, just from knowing that someone of his stature could, or would, appreciate my work. I will be forever grateful to this wonderful musician and human being.

SIDEBAR: At a lunch with Jester a few years later, he shared the concept of "Telegraph Songs" with me, which both my "Mary Had a Baby" and "Wade in the Water" arrangements utilized. The idea is that slaves used these songs as a way to communicate the best time to try and escape to the Freedom Train. In the case of "Mary Had a Baby," the slave owners would drink heavily on the days leading up to Christmas, which made those days a good time to leave. But once Christmas Day came (when Mary had her baby), it was considered too late…"the train has gone." "Wade In The Water" encouraged escaping when the waters became muddy…"God's a-gonna trouble the water" as it would conceal any crossing of the river.

Fred Bock
"Cheap, Tawdry, Contrived, Predictable and Overblown"

I don't think that Fred would consider himself a "choral master" but believe me, he was very talented! Few are aware that the pipe organ music at Disney's Haunted Mansion was indeed recorded by the late Fred Bock. For those even older, he was the producer of the legendary Mrs. Miller and her recording of "Downtown" in the 1960s.

Fred was also a born comedian. His forewords in the "Bock's Best" piano books are a hoot. I had admired his work since I began teaching in the early 1970s when I stumbled on his "Child in a Manger" set to the folk tune of "Morning Has Broken." His vocal lines were very singable and accompaniments tasty.

Fred and I met in Denver at a reading session for Joe Keith at Music Mart and immediately hit it off as we both enjoyed irreverent humor. Below you will see a photocopy of a note he left for me years later when we were staying at the same hotel in Dallas. It says so much!

"Dear Mr. Emerson…Your arrangements are cheap, tawdry, overblown and predictable…my choir LOVES them!
Signed…A friend."

The fact is…humor goes a long way and we should use it with each other and our singers often. We should take what we DO seriously, but not hold ourselves in the same weight.

Dear Mr. Emerson:
Your choral arrangements are cheap, tawdry, contrived, predictable, overblown. My choir loves them!
A friend

RESERVATIONS WORLDWIDE 800-333-3333

Thanks, Fred…I'll continue writing my cheap, tawdry, overblown and predictable arrangements just for you! :)

"I know what a sextet is but I'd rather not say."

5th Grader

Rodney Eichenberger
*"A Handout, a PowerPoint
and a Demonstration Group"*

I met Rod in 1970 when I was a student of Kirby Shaw's at College of the Siskiyous in Weed, California. That's right…Weed…named after the founder of the lumbering town, Abner Weed. Needless to say, particularly lately, the community has capitalized on its moniker, but I digress….

Rod was conducting a countywide choral festival and, as a college student, I was assigned various duties tending to kids and providing water for the clinician, etc. Speaking of water…I remember Rod taking a break and he was drenched with sweat. I was a first-year student and had no idea how much energy one puts into a festival of 200 students, particularly in our rural area…a real challenge.

I followed Rod's career from the University of Washington to USC and, ultimately, to Florida State and, of course, bought all of his books and videotapes and attended every workshop that I could. I learned so much from him, but the most important lesson was perhaps one of the simplest things a director could do to improve the choir: *Spread the singers out.*

There is a tendency, particularly among novice singers, to stand close together for security. Spreading them out lets the sound *breathe*, looks better and fosters independence. Whenever I adjudicate a festival, it is one of the first things that I do and I owe it all to Rod!

SIDEBAR: A few years ago I conducted the "Boot Camp" at California Music Educators Annual Conference. It was an intensive half-day event that really worked on the nuts and bolts of building choral skill. I was quite apprehensive as normally a "choral master" was chosen to preside. James Jordan conducted the year before and Rod the year after me. Funny thing…I was so prepared (out of fear I would not measure up), that I had a handout, a demonstration group and a PowerPoint! When Rod gave his presentation the following year, he said, "I feel so unprepared! Roger had a handout, PowerPoint and a demonstration group!" The fact is, Rod didn't need it…I DID! :)

Charlene Archibeque
"Air Is Everything"

For those who do not know this "choral master," if I remember correctly, she was the first woman to receive a doctorate in choral conducting and was an icon for over 40 years at San Jose State University in Northern California. I met her early in her career...in 1976, if I recall. She had been recruited to teach a one-day clinic at our local high school. This school of about 300 had a fledging but earnest program and director, but results were generally just okay.

I spent part of the day watching Charlene work and was so impressed by her command. Her attention to breath and its use to propel the musical line was enlightening and is the reason that I now always say, "Air is everything!"

I could only stay for an hour that day, as I had my own teaching responsibilities, but made a point to attend the evening concert. WOW! Chills! The ensemble had become truly exciting in ONE day under Charlene's leadership. The takeaway for me was that kids are kids. With the proper leadership and expert instruction, they can all be amazing. Thank you, Charlene Archibeque... you are truly a "choral master."

Edith Copley
"Disco Fever"

A few years ago at our annual California Choral Directors Association (CCDA) Summer Conference at ECCO (Episcopal Conference Center, Oakhurst), there was a great deal of buzz about our headliner: Edie Copley. Everyone said, "You'll love her…she's so good and so real." So, of course, I was really looking forward to her sessions.

They were right…she WAS amazing. So knowledgeable, practical and down to earth. At the end of the first plenary session, I went up to her and said, "Ms. Copley, it's so good to meet you. Your session was so helpful and I learned so much. Thank you!" Her response was priceless:

"Roger! Don't you remember that we disco-danced in 1980 at ICDA (Iowa Choral Directors Association) in Mason City, Iowa!?" I dug deep and did remember the fun and dancing at that local watering hole, but had no idea that it was her! Embarrassed I was, but glad that we had shared this connection, and that we continue to have a connection.

So, what did I learn from this "choral master"? That the reason she was so good is that she had started humbly in rural Iowa and truly understood where the rest of us were coming from. This is not always true, but certainly was in her case. A year or two later, I had the opportunity to hear her ensemble from NAU (Northern Arizona University) and I realized something else. Her years of junior high and high school teaching made her a terrific programmer. Her pieces were beautifully paced and always kept the audience engaged. Sometimes, choral music can be so esoteric that it is appreciated but not enjoyed. It's a good lesson to learn.

"Refrain means don't do it! A refrain in music is the part you'd better not play."

5th Grader

Joshua Habermann
"Butter"

It was one of those fall kick-off regional conferences. The attendance was light but enthusiastic and the workshops were practical and varied. Josh was the "headliner" for the day. Young, talented and fun to listen to. But on this day, he demonstrated a concept that I had struggled with for years: how to properly explain a flipped "r" used, for instance, in the word "gloria" when sung in Latin.

"Butter." Say it... "Butter." Sense where the tongue touches the roof of the mouth. It's perfect, simple and easily shared with choir members. GLORIA! (See the companion article next regarding the "o" in Latin!)

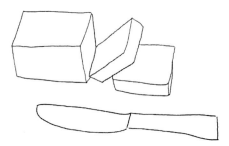

William Hall
"AW"

 I knew that my mom's cousin Oakley Allred sang in a professional chorus, but it wasn't until years later when I became a choral director myself that I realized he sang in the *William Hall Chorale*! I guess choir is in my blood!

For years I was baffled by those pronunciation guides that are offered with the Latin text of a choral piece that would indicate "gloria" should be pronounced "GLAW-ria." To me, it never made sense that the "o" would be so buried in the back of the throat. Bill Hall explained it so much better than a pronunciation guide ever could… It is "o" without its diphthong "oo." Say it… "Oh-oo." Now without the "oo."

THAT is how the "o" in "gloria" should be properly sung in Latin. Simple and effective.

> SIDEBAR: I was chatting with Bill at an ACDA Conference a few years ago and he lamented that in the movie, *Sister Act 2*, his Chapman Choir portrayed a high school choir that competed with Whoopi Goldberg's ensemble and lost out to them…of course…it's a movie! Each group had performed Beethoven's "Ode to Joy," his a straight-ahead version and Whoopi's quite hip. Although he was disappointed, it was still great press and I assume that it made him or the university a nice chunk of change!

Joyce Eilers
"Where Have You Been All My Life"

I first became familiar with Joyce through her early choral works designed for middle school. I really struggled with my first middle school (mixed 7-8) choir. The kids were terrific and I had over 50 of them, but my literature choices were just not appropriate. I often say they sang a new voicing…soprano/alto/mud.

The bari-tenors, as I like to call them, were all over the place until I stumbled on a piece by Joyce called "Brighten My Soul with Sunshine." Suddenly the mud went away and they sounded like a choir! I met Joyce the following summer and played my pieces "Sinner Man" and "First, We Must Be Friends" for her.

The response? "Where have you been all my life?!" She called her friend Art Jenson at Hal Leonard who promised to "do what he could" for her young friend. Six months later when Art formed his own company, Jenson Publications, I was the first one he called. The rest is history, for which I will always be grateful. More importantly, what I learned from Joyce was the importance of mentoring. For those who know me, I don't hesitate to pass on to a publisher an exciting piece of music that comes across my desk. I've also mentored guitar students and collaborated with young Matt Cleveland in the creation of *S'COOL - A Teenage Pop/Rock Musical*. Quite frankly, through these efforts, I often learn more than my students. Thanks, Joyce, for this valuable lesson.

"A virtuoso is somebody with real high morals."

4th Grader

Jean Ashworth Bartle
"Unison"

Truth is, I've never met Ms. Bartle, but her ensemble, The Toronto Children's Chorus, had an epic impact on me years ago at an ACDA convention in San Diego.

I have always been a fan of harmony, particularly modern jazz harmony: thick and rich with dissonance. But on this day, at a conference known for wonderful choirs performing amazing choral works, often thick with harmony, I had an epiphany.

The Toronto Children's Chorus performed "Bist Du Bei Mir" by Bach...in UNISON! It was magnificent! The beauty of line and tone were spellbinding. Yes, of course, there was harmony in the accompaniment, but not in the choral rendition. It made me keenly aware that often we choral directors are so drawn to complexity that we forget or ignore the importance of a simple, unison line, performed with excellence.

I will never again fail to appreciate the importance and opportunity that a unison line avails us. I hope you will not either.

William Dehning
"No"

"No, no,no,no,no, etc."

I only met Bill Dehning a few years ago and at that time he was in failing health, but I feel as though I know him from his wonderful book *Chorus Confidential*. (Full disclosure: It's published by my book publisher, Pavane. Please buy it because it's a great, practical read and Allan Petker could use the money!)

I gleaned a simple technique that has proved quite useful from the book: When you have a *melisma,* such as "gloria" in "Angels We Have Heard On High," have a portion of the choir place a voiced consonant such as "n" before each note of the melisma to give definition to the line. Glo,no,no,no,no,no,no,no,no,no,no,ria! It will work nicely...think of the many uses of being able to say "no" with such success! Go!

Henry Leck
"Falsetto"

My first introduction to Henry's work was through a video of his amazing Indianapolis Children's Chorus. Not only were they fun to watch (I learned later this movement was carefully choreographed) but more importantly, they had a free and "natural" sound to their voices. I often find select children's choirs to sound somewhat sterile, and his was anything but. I said to myself, "THAT'S the way a kid's choir ought to sound…and look for that matter." Please YouTube the ensemble when able and let it be the benchmark for all of us who teach youth choir.

In addition, I had the opportunity to teach with him a few times and I was somewhat taken aback by his suggestion that monotones (or "uncertain singers" as Joyce Eilers liked to call them) could often match pitch in falsetto when they were unable to in full voice. Try it! It works! I have since learned that Don Brinegar also advocates this technique.

In closing, just so you know, we don't have to agree. Henry's choirs always do the same warm-up…seems odd to me as I like to fashion the warm-up to achieve some goal within the literature itself. I assume his kids are so good they probably don't need it! Still lots of respect for his marvelous work.

"Beethoven expired in 1827 ... and later died from it."

4th Grader

Tim Seelig
"Words Are Everything"

If you haven't read Tim's book *Big Ol' Baptist, Big Ol' Gay*...please do. It's a hoot and will reveal more of both his humor and his humanity. Tim is a marvelous clinician and has a heavenly voice...he has that Baptist thing, and growing up in the church I suppose didn't hurt. A simple technique I learned from him is to take a phrase and underline (have the choir underline) the important words in a phrase. Then give them a little more emPHAsis when singing the line. It's an amazing transformation in phrasing and SO simple!

How many times do we jump right into the music without taking time to explore the text first? In fact, it would be ideal to jump in without even seeing the notes. You'd be surprised at what a difference it makes not only in interpretation, but also in singer "buy-in" when we commence a new piece with this most important concept. Thanks Tim...you're my favorite Big Ol' Baptist, Big Ol' Gay!

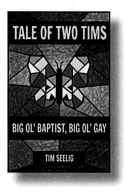

Pat Patton
"Messa Di Voce"

Just a few years ago, at our annual California Choral Directors Association (CCDA) Summer Conference at ECCO (Episcopal Conference Center, Oakhurst), I first met Pat and Marcia Patton, as they were the headliners. Anyone in Wyoming knows this talented and gracious couple, as they are CHOIR WYOMING!

My undergraduate degree in voice was, well, underwhelming, perhaps because I was not ready to learn or the institution as a whole was just...okay. Either way, I have played a lot of catch-up over the years and have never stopped my joy of learning. Pat's main emphasis was on the importance of *messa di voce* in vocal training, health and performance. I had often used this concept of crescendo/decrescendo on one note as a warm-up exercise, but had never put the term and the practice together. The reality is that even quarter notes can have this rise and fall that will help propel the phrase along beautifully.

My point...the joy of being a music educator is that there is always more to learn and NOBODY knows it all...not even the most esteemed choral conductor. Keep learning!

Jefferson Johnson
"Bluegrass"

I first recognized Jeff's talent while watching his video, "Ready, Set, Sing!" as his advice was so practical and effective. I was even more impressed when I had the opportunity to hear and see his University of Kentucky Men's Chorus at National ACDA in Chicago in 2011. These guys sang with amazing passion and I just knew that it reflected their amazing director.

Just a few years later, I had the opportunity to conduct a workshop with him and was truly struck by his "down-home" demeanor. Equally as fascinating was his passion for Bluegrass music and in particular The Wailin' Jennys. It just goes to show that those we most admire often have very eclectic tastes in music. Very few listen to Bach motets on a regular basis... thank goodness!

SIDEBAR: On that same program I was taken with the National ACDA Men's Chorus Performing "Rainbow 'Round My Shoulder" under Peter Bagley. They used chains as called for in the choral but expanded it to include many in the chorus, downstage with chains... truly fascinating. I later realized that the piece was arranged and adapted by my friend, Robert DeCormier, whom I had recently dined with during a Hal Leonard reading session. He was a passionate progressive and musical director for Peter, Paul and Mary who passed in 2017 at the ripe old age of 95!

"Chopin had many fast friends, but the fastest was Miss George Sands."

5th Grader

Jeffrey Benson
"Scissorhands"

I'm not sure where or when we first met, but I knew I liked Jeffrey from the beginning. How could a guy who looked 18 be so damn good?! I find myself saying that about quite a few of the new, young directors out there. Quite frankly, across the board they have been better trained than my generation, and I think the appearance of high school ensembles that sound like the college choirs of yesteryear is a testament to that fact.

Just recently I watched Jeffery conduct a session in which he applied the concepts of Dalcroze that we all use when we apply a physical gesture to our teaching, but it was simple…. Use and have your singers use the index and middle finger to create a crescendo and decrescendo wedge as a symbol to rise and fall the phrase. It's magic, and that's just one of many of his ideas.

With any luck my editor will spring for a few extra pages for Jeffery's priceless handout with over 50 tips for improving your choir. Remember: Surround yourself with people who are better than you. Funny thing…it always works!

Handout provided at the end of this book.
You're welcome, Roger
– *Allan*

Christine Bass
"Work Those Abs, Baby"

Christine Bass is the real deal. If you haven't watched her two videos, "Vocal Transformation" and "Front-Loading Your Choral Rehearsal," (Hal Leonard Publishing), you are missing out on seeing what quality, systematic application of skills can do to make a bunch of high school singers into a choir. I also love her because she routinely features a few of my pieces in her workshops… 😎 Even more important to me is that she is a wonderful technician who is not afraid to share improvements in thought with this old guy.

You know the old phrase "sing from the diaphragm"? Well, of course, with my sense of humor, this always makes me chuckle. Well, the concept is WRONG…the diaphragm is an involuntary muscle that floats at the pleasure of the abdominals! So, perhaps, we should all say "sing from your abs." Carry on.

Don Brinegar
"Brilliance Close to Home"

Only recently have I gotten to know Don, who is perhaps the most brilliant technician in our choral field. He and I grew up in Southern California at about the same time, but as I grew in pop and jazz, he progressed in the intricacies of conducting, the voice and choir intonation. We are Facebook friends (I know there are downsides to social media, but there are also many pluses), and he shares posts regarding the theory behind a variety of subjects, including how chords properly tune, how changing voices can find their way utilizing falsetto and many more well-researched and carefully thought-out topics. I highly recommend reading his various treatises.

takefivewithprofessordon.blog

"Johann Sebastian Bach died from 1750 to the present."

4th Grader

Jo-Michael Scheibe
"Let It Float"

Mike Scheibe, Don Brinegar and I are contemporaries who grew up just miles from one another, but our paths could not be more divergent. I was always immersed in popular music and they, of course, were/are choral giants. Had I attended Long Beach State (now California State University at Long Beach) under Frank Pooler or Chapman College under William Hall, I might too be a "choral giant," but alas it was not to be. I'm not really sure I have the right stuff, quite frankly.

Only recently, through my association with CCDA (California Choral Directors Association) have I had the privilege to work with with brilliant people like Mike and Don. We choir people never stop learning and I gleaned an important concept from Mike a few years ago during a joint appearance at a Conductor's Craft workshop. I have made an honest effort to fill in the gaps in my choral education every chance that I get, and at this workshop I was explaining the importance of posture, air and an elevated rib cage. Mike was kind enough to take me aside after my session to stress the importance of letting the rib cage float and not remain raised and static. Thanks, Mike, for sharing this most important aspect of breathing!

Paul Salamunovich
"Nothing New Under the Sun"

I first met Paul in 1980 at the Choral Arts Seminar of the Rockies in Estes Park, Colorado. Brilliant and approachable, he was great and we hit it off immediately. His expertise in Gregorian Chant was legendary and his workshop was illuminating. As a young conductor and composer, I was fascinated by the nuance of the genre that he shared.

Years later, he and I sat together at ACDA Washington at the premier of the Moses Hogan Chorale. I just remember him smiling and saying, "They're pretty good!" If I remember correctly, he also said, "There's nothing new under the sun." I think he had witnessed firsthand the rise of the music of William Dawson and the music and expertise of Jester Hairston and knew that, although this fabulous new voice was important, spirituals and their impact are legendary. I miss you, Paul, and am so glad that we were friends.

Andre Thomas
"Trip the Light Fantastic"

Andre and I met briefly years ago when he was conducting an honor choir in nearby Sacramento, California. If I recall, I bought him dinner...I guess I should ask him if he remembers! We are, of course, Facebook friends and often say "hope our paths cross," and they did a few years ago when he was the keynote speaker at our Northern California CCDA Fall Conference.

In his address, he spoke of the challenges of his first choral job in the St. Louis area and how he was thrown into the most challenging group of students in the district. It may have been all tenor/basses if I recall and they really didn't want to be there...sound familiar?

The way he was finally able to get them to engage was through a light show. That's right, a light show. He was able to commandeer those speakers that change colors according to the frequency being omitted. As off-the-wall as this was in a "choral" setting, he realized that establishing a rapport was critical if he was ever going to get them to sing, which he eventually did.

My takeaway? Everybody, even the finest conductors, starts somewhere...usually at the bottom and work up. In addition, his ability to "solve the problem" in a creative and engaging way set the tone for the remainder of his career. I am humbled to be called his friend.

"Bach is the most famous composer in the world and so is Handel. By the way, Handel was half German, half Italian and half English...he was rather large."

5th Grader

Anton Armstrong
"Grace"

I had heard through the grapevine that Anton (famed conductor at St. Olaf) was not a fan of my contemporary settings of spirituals and when I met him, I was, in fact, quite intimidated. But the reality is that if he felt that way, it never showed. He was and is the epitome of kindness and grace in addition to being a choral master.

I have often thought about how I treat people with whom I don't see eye to eye, and when I'm tempted to cold-shoulder them, I think of Anton…kindness, grace, take the high road. We are all better for it.

Morton Lauridsen
"Don't 'Skip' the Melody"

Clever me…a play on Morton's nickname, Skip. We only know each other in passing… We have a "Hi, how are you?" kind of association, but I've got to tell you, I am a REAL fan. I love contemporary choral music with those lush chords and rich clusters, but some of it leaves me cold. I can appreciate it, but I don't enjoy it.

Morton's work is different. Not only are there incredible, rich, contemporary harmonies, but more importantly… melodies. I'm a firm believer that it is melodies that stand the test of time. Think of Beethoven's 9th or Handel's Messiah or even Rodgers and Hammerstein. What we remember are the melodies. I am convinced that Morton "Skip" Lauridsen's music will stand the test of time because of it. We can only hope.

John Rutter
"Across the Pond"

I just recently ran across a letter that I had received from John that acknowledged receipt of my condolences on the passing of his son at the age of 23. Truly tragic, but I have a lighter remembrance of John, who is a brilliant writer.

I've always loved his "Blow, Blow, Thou Winter Wind" and "For the Beauty of the Earth." They are two of my all-time favorite choral pieces. Years ago, when I started my career somewhat concurrently with his, we both would be featured on various reading sessions. At the time, my publisher, Jenson Publications, believed that if you charged more for a workshop, the sponsors felt like they were getting more. I was perhaps the highest paid at $400/day in 1980.

When John requested the same and was rebuffed, he purportedly said, "Even Roger Emerson gets $400 a day!"

Quite frankly, if I was worth $400 (somewhat debatable), John was worth double that! Every time I think about it I have to smile. I'm just glad John Rutter knows who I am! ☺

Eric Whitacre
"More Than the Hair"

I don't know Eric well, but admire his work and, even more, his promotional sense and ability to build an amazing image. If you haven't seen his European luggage print ads, you're missing out. Some years ago he was signing autographs at a music conference and the line of young people stretched down the aisle. As I passed by, he looked up and said, "Roger, we need to get together." I'm still waiting.

We would probably discuss our history playing in rock 'n' roll bands, he in Reno, me in Los Angeles. I'll let you know. Meanwhile, I've made an appointment for some locks from Hair Club For Men so that I too can have a long line for my book signing!

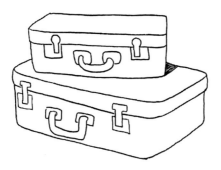

"Johann Sebastian Bach had 20 children. In the attic he had a spinster on which he practiced!" ☺

Grade withheld by request

Dale Warland
"If That's Not a Cluster"

Whoa! Not the one you're thinking! I had the pleasure of meeting Dale at the Jenson Choral Arts Seminar of the Rockies organized by Jim Kimmel. Dale is one of the kindest men you will ever meet and I soon realized he and I had an affinity for cluster chords long before Morton Lauridsen and Eric Whitacre.

His first album of Christmas arrangements is one of my favorites and when I heard it, I realized that it was fine to have luscious dissonance be a part of choral music and it was right up my alley as a jazz buff. Here's to many more clusters!! The good kind.

Frank Pooler
"Merry Christmas, Roger"

I grew up in Downey, California, home of The Carpenters and, although we are contemporaries, Karen and Richard went to a rival high school and we never met. However, I often wonder how my life would have been different had I attended Long Beach State College under the direction of Frank Pooler and in association with Richard and Karen. I actually didn't meet Frank until well into my composing/arranging career and never spent time with The Carpenters.

Frank was an imposing figure to me; however, once I met him, I realized how gracious a man he was in real life. For some reason, he took a liking to me and would send beautiful holiday greetings each year along with a rendering of his artwork. (Yep…he was an amazing artist as well.) I guess the takeaway is to never judge a book by its cover. Although he could be a terror on the podium, he was truly a kind and gentle soul.

SIDEBAR: We all get to enjoy a Christmas card of sorts from Frank in his wonderful lyrics to "Merry Christmas, Darling." Recently I learned he wrote the lyrics 20 years prior to Richard's music. I guess good things do come to those who wait!

Rollo Dilworth
"I'm Taking Credit for Your Career!"

I met Rollo (btw…it's RAH-LO not ROH-LO…although he is a sweet guy!) in 1995 at an Oklahoma ACDA Conference hosted by Cristi Miller (Cris-tee not Cristie). ☺ We were picked up at the hotel and sat together in the back seat enroute to the conference. The first thing he did is lean over and say, "I sang your music in junior high!" Now, some people would be offended at the unintended implication that I was old…hell, I know that!

But rather, I was flattered knowing that in some small way my music was part of the musical fabric of this talented and iconic composer. Rollo, you're sweet like Rolo, only better and I'm so glad we are friends!

Stephen Schwartz
"Out of Context"

I learned every song off of two albums in my life...
okay...three: *Oklahoma*, the 1957 movie, Crosby, Stills
and Nash's first album, and "Godspell: Original Cast"
album.

Stephen Schwartz is a true tunesmith, as much as
Rodgers and Hammerstein...that's why we remember
their melodies.

The "Godspell: the Original Cast" album also reveals
a little-known fact: Paul Shaffer, who was for a year the
band leader on *Saturday Night Live,* was the musical
director. I miss album covers and all of their interesting
info. For years, I would look for producers and musical
directors that I liked, as opposed to artists, because
I knew that the album would have the sensibility
and sound of the producer. Michael Omartian is one
example, the producer of Christopher Cross and many
other albums. Always tasty. I digress.

I've had the pleasure of meeting Stephen on several
occasions, but he and I had a real disagreement on
my arrangement of "Defying Gravity" from *Wicked*. If
you recall, the ending from the show has that stunning
contrary motion with the words... "So, we've got
to bring her down!" and it closes the first act. My
arrangement included that fabulous ending. Mac Huff
had done the recording and it was stellar, but Stephen
wanted it re-recorded with the ending you will now
find on the choral.

His rationale: "It's out of context." We emailed back and forth, with me trying to convince him that choirs and their directors would want the big ending, but he would not budge and who am I to tell Stephen Schwartz what to do? I was tempted to say… "It's a choral setting…the entire thing is out of context!" but I was afraid he would pull the entire piece so…sorry, folks…I tried.

SIDEBAR: Funny thing…a few years later I did a nice ballad arrangement of "Beautiful City" and he sent a note saying it was the most lovely vocal arrangement he had ever heard. I'll take it! ☺

"As one grows older they can be one of two things...a dinosaur or a Yoda."

Roger Emerson - Grade wisely withheld

The Hal Leonard
Gang - L to R
Ed Lojeski,
Mac Huff,
Emily Crocker,
John Jacobson,
John Leavitt,
Roger (seated)
- 2000

Roger's mom's 3 cousins,
L to R - Oakley Allred (who
sang with Wm. Hall), Lucille
Smith and Doris Allred, who
sang on live radio and mom
arranged their music.
- 1936

The "Little Blue Notes," Downey High School
students performing in 1936.

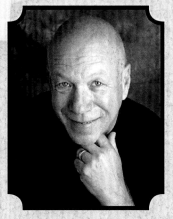

Roger Emerson
- 2012

Hal Leonard
Arrangers -
L to R (seated)
Mac Huff,
Rollo Dilworth,
(standing)
John Jacobson,
Cristi Miller,
Roger
- 2015

The Emerson Family
L to R
Kayla, Roger,
Mari, Ryder
- 2015

Northern California
ACDA - L to R
Jeffery Benson,
Roger,
Andre Thomas
- 2014

Partners in Chime
Roger and
Greg Eastman
- 2014

ACDA National Salt
Lake City
L to R - Roger,
Rollo Dilworth,
Cristi Miller
- 2014

Roger with
brothers - L to R -
Randy Derwingson,
Roger,
Richard Derwingson
- 2000

Roger and Mari
- 1980

Roger and
daughter Kayla
- 2020

Roger and Mari
Birthday Ski
- 2012

Roger with step dad Jim Emerson Camping - 2016

The New York Voices

Ruthevelyn Smith Emerson - 1950

Roger
with Jack Zaino
- 2021

James and Ruthevelyn
Emerson
- 1965

Roger
- 1980

Writer's Retreat
- L to R - Rollo
Dilworth, Linda
Schmidt
(J.W. Pepper),
Mac Huff,
David Leytus,
Audrey Snyder
- 2017

Roger,
Kirby Shaw,
John Jacobson
- 2014

The Emerson
Canine Collection
- L to R - Spanky,
Wrigley, Pablo,
Frankie and Izzy
- 2016

Roger and
Alan Billingsley
- 2020

Ryder Kole Emerson
- 2017

Head's House of Music
Reading Session
Front row - L to R
Robert DeCormier,
Roger Wagner,
Milton Gould,
Back row - Roger,
Julie Knowles,
Bill Head
- 1991

Part II

The Friends

Also Masters in Their Own Way

(In alphabetical order to protect the innocent
and keep me out of trouble!)

Jerry Anderson
"It's All About Airstream"

No, this chapter is not about trailers! For any band directors reading this book, you might recognize this name as one of the authors of "Standards of Excellence" Band Method. He is a wonderful and talented clinician and is married to the famed Linda Allen Anderson, who taught junior high for years in Santa Monica and produced one of those choirs that sang like a college choir and made you want to give up teaching for good…that good!

I was paired with Jerry at a festival in Southern California where he would clinic the bands and I, the choirs. As usual, I listened intently to his comments to see if I could dovetail with his theme. He said something profound that seems so simple, but is so important to both vocalists and instrumentalists: "It's all about airstream."

As simple a concept as this is, it is critical to a full, vibrant and beautiful sound. "Air." Many vocal issues can be solved by making sure that not only are students taking a breath, but are then using it effectively. Lip buzzes work well for this…it's impossible to buzz your lips without a full breath and moving air. In instrumental music, the idea of filling with air and then articulating with the tongue creates beautiful connected phrases. Ever heard a band or choir that punches every quarter note? Or a lackluster whole note? Think this: A whole note is merely four quarter-notes tied together. This idea that a whole note is not static but must have motion has changed my thinking about motion of the phrase and the notes within. Try it! Thanks, Jerry and Linda, who probably gave him the idea!! :)

Alan Billingsley
"Party Animal"

This description couldn't be further from the truth, but you'll find out why I titled this chapter this way. Alan is a consummate musician, having been musical director for the likes of Johnny Mathis, Denise Williams, James Darren and more.

He and I met when we were both 30 and he was not only best man at my wedding, but producer of the bulk of my recordings and musicals since then. Musically, he taught me the importance of accuracy when recording, click tracks, 3rd passes, synth pads, buttons and more. I'll be forever grateful for the studio experience with him.

So...where does "Party Animal" come in? Shortly after we met, we went skiing outside Denver, and on our way back to the airport he suggested that we stop at an accountant friend's get-together. We did and it was attended by mostly accountants and attorneys who, instead of drinking beer, were smoking pot. The funny thing is the two musicians in the room, he and I, never touched the stuff! We have often gotten a laugh out of that.

My association with Alan has certainly been fun and I've learned a lot, but in addition to the somewhat ironic episode above, my favorite adventure was being dragged along to Richard Marx' Showcase at a club in Los Angeles called Sasha, circa 1986. For those unfamiliar with what a showcase is, it's when a new artist, seeking a record deal, puts on a live concert for A&R (artist and repertoire) people from the various record companies, movers and shakers in the industry, etc. Alan knew Richard's dad, Dick Marks from Chicago, as he owned a studio where we produced our early recordings, including the first *TEEN* album.

What I didn't expect was that the movers and shakers would include Lionel Richie, Barry Manilow, David Foster and Donnie Osmond, among many others…I was so starstruck that I failed to take names. It was an amazing evening, but for me, the best part was chatting with Donnie's wife, Debbie. While others were fawning over her husband, I sauntered up and said, "Hey, I met your dad, Avery Glenn, a few weeks ago while conducting in Utah!" Her father was Supervisor of Music for Utah Public Schools and we had met during a conference in Salt Lake. I think she loved that someone would chat with her as she waited patiently for her husband. Donnie came over, however, and gave me the evil eye until I mentioned Avery…it was quite a night and one I will never forget. Thanks, Al!

Ted Bluechel
"Not Ready for Prime Time"

At 18, I began doing studio work in Los Angeles playing electric bass. I had been recruited by a producer who had heard me play live with my rock band, The Nervous System…don't ask…I didn't pick the name! One of the hottest groups at the time was The Association, who had hits like "Along Comes Mary" and "Cherish," and I got a call to do the "demo" session of a song for their next album. Of course, I was flattered and nervous. In reality, I had good ears, could read chord symbols and simple notation, but was nowhere ready for the demands of the studio.

When I got to the studio and was setting up, the drummer, Ted Bluechel, looked over at me and said, "You're so young." I don't hear that phrase much these days! ☺ The next thing was that the producer put music in front of me and it was notation, high in the register and, quite frankly, paralyzing! I somehow managed to make it work, but was never called back. I realized then and there that I was not ready for prime time and that studio playing was not going to be my career. It was fun to be asked, however, and as Eleanor Roosevelt said, "Do something that scares you every day."

Mark Brymer
"There's No Business"

Mark is not only a gifted arranger and producer who is always on the cutting edge, but also the consummate business man. Few are aware of his work outside of education, which includes creating amazing theme-park shows and co-writing a tune in Disney's *101 Dalmatians.* He has become Dolly Parton's right hand man...oh, and he co-wrote the *Juke Box Musicals* with MTI and is currently penning a Broadway show. Get busy, Mark!!

I have learned so much about the business side of music from him. I think perhaps all music educators should become familiar with the business side of music and education. It drives everything from ADA (Average Daily Attendance), the funding driver for schools, to one's yearly music budget. Nothing funny to add here...it's just good business!

SIDEBAR: Just a few years ago, thanks to social media, I learned that Mark and I were in New York at the same time to see a few shows. Sure enough, we met up at Joe Allen (famous NY eatery) for a late dinner. It was an evening I won't forget because we never seem to get the chance to do that type of thing together despite having a 30-year association. Coincidental and spontaneous...the best kind of night!

Chet Christiansen
"By the Power Vested in Me"

Principals ALWAYS have money. You just have to figure out how to get it. Chet was not necessarily the most effective administrator I ever worked for, but his simple, validating gesture is perhaps the most memorable of my 40 years in education.

I taught for a total of 12 years at the middle-school level and loved it…but it's the hardest job you'll ever love. Around my fifth year, our school instituted a new set of popular electives, which diminished my 50-voice 7-8 grade choir to 17! Holy cow! My first impulse was to turn the class into a guitar class, but I had an epiphany that these 17 wanted to sing more than any other thing and I owed it to them to give them my utmost best. I had planned new uniforms (vests and ties), a tour to the Bay Area for an exchange concert and a trip to the Great America Theme Park and a local tour. At first I thought…scrap it!

Fortunately, I came to my senses and proceeded to move forward. Well, as you can imagine, the new elective offerings soon became stale and word got out that the choir was doing some fun things. Here is where Chet comes in…second quarter my choir number jumped to 34, and I went to him and said, "We have a problem, I need more money for uniforms." I'll never forget his reply, "You get the kids, I'll get the vests!" Music to my ears and a response that represents the power that an administrator has to validate what you are doing. By the way, we ended the year with 60. Hallelujah!

"If you expect your friends to be perfect, you won't have many friends."

Roger Emerson - Grade complicated

Emily Crocker
"The Queen of Choral"

Emily and I are the same age, born two weeks apart and are both Capricorns. You know what that means: We are both RIGHT! It has led to some fun negotiations and sometimes agreeing to disagree.

Our musical *Zombies the Musical* was one such project. She just didn't feel at the time it was "appropriate" for Hal Leonard. At the time, she was probably right, but a few years later Disney premiered their movie, Z-O-M-B-I-E-S, and once that happens, the gloves are off. Well, John Jacobson and I went on to self-publish the show, which has been quite successful and if you'd like to hear it, go to allschoolmusic.com.

Where she and I will never disagree is on the impact that her leadership has had on the choral community. A diminutive Texan, her work with expanding the scope of Hal Leonard, Essential Elements, McGraw Hill textbooks and The Milwaukee Childrens Chorus is legendary. She is truly the queen of choral.

P.S. Don't mess with a Texan or a Cappy!

Ireta Cushing
"The Eyes Have It"

Ireta was my elementary music teacher and first choir teacher, grades 5 and 6. I still use her ideas about focus and intonation to this day. Choir was only once a week during lunch, so for those of you who lament how little time you have with your singers, just remember she turned out this composer/arranger "in about an hour" at Choircrafters. One never knows the impact one has on kids. We all know the troublemakers and the high achievers but those kids in the middle are equally absorbent, like a good paper towel.

Ireta was a devout Mormon, but as a traveling music teacher (I think she had five schools), she needed her pick-me-up. Her drink of choice was a bottle (that's right, drinks used to come in bottles) of Pepsi that she would slam down on the old Baldwin piano before beginning warm-ups. Her cue to watch her was always "eyes"…and you would incur "that look" if you deviated…being a bit of a deviant myself and somewhat ADHD, I got those looks quite often. I also learned that raising the eyebrows would raise the soft pallet and aid in raising a sagging pitch, particularly on an SA reduction of the bridge of the Wilhousky "Battle Hymn of the Republic." "In the beauty of the lilies…" You know the rest. The combined festival chorus marked my entrance to the choir world, my first sport coat and very fond memories of this amazing educator.

Greg Eastman
"Co-Conspirators"

Yep…we ganged up on singing in Mount Shasta and won! When I resigned from teaching at our local high school, we went through a series of directors, a few quite good, but most not so, until we hired Greg Eastman. Like me, he is a natural musician who likes kids (a great start for any choir director) and, collectively, we have grown. For him, the beginning was when I dragged him to his first ACDA. Bingo… he went from programming Lojeski, Albrecht, and Emerson, to Lauridsen, Whitacre and Gjeilo!

He and I volunteered at the middle school for a year to revive the program. We team-taught and it was a blast…those kids didn't know what hit them. We liked to call the rehearsal "Ham and Eggin'." If you haven't done it with a colleague, try it. Just about the time you are running out of ideas, your partner comes up with a fix. I wish every mixed ensemble had a soprano/alto and tenor/bass with which to model performance and team-teach. Just imagine.

In closing, a concept that I think Greg gleaned from his instrumental instruction was, "Never leave a long sound alone." Long notes should generally either grow or diminish. Doing so quite naturally propels the phrase. Whatever we are doing or have done seems to be working…our little town of 3,500 was able to boast 66 percent of its students in an elective performing arts program in a survey conducted by the California Department of Education several years ago. It's a team effort of community support, money and scheduling. Greg retires this year, but as we all know, music educators seldom really retire. I'm just glad he was my partner in crime all these years...I meant "chime" all these "ears."

Lloyd Elliot
"A Sustained Sigh"

Lloyd Elliot was a colleague at College of the Siskiyous where I studied under Kirby Shaw and eventually taught. He reminded me a bit of John Haussman, the actor from the *FAME* television series. Brilliant, well educated, intimidating. Lloyd received his degree from University of the Pacific and sang under Bill Dehning, so he had "good chops," as we say, and an excellent pedigree.

I've always felt that sometimes we overanalyze singing when it should be simple, free and natural. Lloyd and I would often discuss vocal technique, but one day he said something that really resonated with me and I often use the idea with my students: "Singing is merely a sustained sigh." Breathe, sigh, sustain a pitch on the way down. Simple, effective and something every singer can do. Try it! It works!

Brendan Graham
"You Raise Me Up"

I'm often asked if I get to meet the people whose work I arrange and, on occasion I do, but not often. When the song "You Raise Me Up" performed by Josh Groban, produced by David Foster, first came out, I was thrilled to get the assignment to create a choral setting. But if you recall, there was only one verse. I felt it needed two and commenced to write a second verse...silly me! I was put in contact with the lyricist, Brendan Graham, who promptly sent me the second verse. I went on to arrange the tune, which is one of my favorites (and also his favorite) of all the arrangements.

He is about my age, lives in Ireland and suggested that if I were ever in New York, I should let him know, as he was often there on business. Sure enough, my next trip was concurrent with his and we arranged a meeting. If I recall, I was staying cheap at The Pod and, of course, he was at The Ritz, as befits a famous writer. He invited me to lunch...steak sandwiches at $50 a pop and we immediately hit it off.

Since then, he has visited our home in California and I was treated to his show *Celtic Woman* in New York. I often get nice notes and, of course, I have promised to visit, but the pandemic has slowed that down a bit. Regardless, his praise and encouragement have always "Raised Me Up" and for that, I am forever grateful.

Janae Green
"Last Dance"

I'm often asked, "What was the most memorable experience of your teaching career?" That is an easy answer...Jenae Green.

I was teaching high school at the time. Since I demanded that all singers in my "pop" ensemble had to also be in concert choir (this is before AP classes), I ended up with 12 soprano/altos and, hence, arranged a lot of SSA literature that year!

One day the school counselor sent a new student to see me. The student was new at the school, very quiet, sullen, large in stature and one of the only POC (people of color) in our school of 300. I asked her if she would like to listen for a day or two to see if this was the class she really wanted. That was Monday... five days later on Friday, she came up to me at the end of class and said, "Mr. Emerson, would you listen to my cassette?" This is many years ago, as you can now tell by the music medium...at least it wasn't an eight-track! I, of course, said yes and she started to play and sing! The song was "Last Dance" by Donna Summer. If you are familiar, it starts rubato and then goes to time. I was FLABBERGASTED! She sounded just like Donna Summer...oh my! Once I recovered, of course, I said, "You're in!" And I proceeded to arrange the tune for her as a solo with my jazz band.

At the next pep rally, this non-descript new student went from Zero to Hero. A spontaneous standing ovation by 300 of her fellow students. I still get chills thinking about how close I came to writing her off. A lesson well learned about our job as educators. Find that hidden talent. It is all around us.

John Higgins
"Convoy"

Some of you might recognize this name, as he is a wonderful orchestrator and arranger of bands, and he was my first boss at Jenson Publications.

People often ask, "Who chooses the pop songs that you arrange?" These days it is a blend of songs that I like that I believe will make a good choral, and songs that are pitched to me to arrange by the publisher... but in the beginning, it was always the publisher.

In this case, it was the novelty tune "Convoy" that is a song, but has a spoken portion with CB radio chatter. At the time, I was reluctant to start, but my big boss, Art Jenson, said, "John can arrange ANYTHING! He sketches his charts in his mind while taking a shower!" Oh my...I wasn't sure that would work for me, but I proceeded to arrange the tune and, believe it or not, it was a hit. I had to learn that sometimes my tastes are irrelevant and, even though I might not program a song, others often will and vice versa.

Mac Huff
"Dogs, Ponies and Me"

The first time I met Mac, he and John Jacobson were leading the Hal Leonard portion of a reading session at Marshall Music in Southern California. It was amazing! At the time, I was the lone clinician for Jenson Publications and, quite frankly, my sessions paled in comparison. I remember saying to myself, "THAT'S the way to demonstrate choral music!" He beautifully played and directed while JJ choreographed the pieces. It was an amazing dog-and-pony show for which I would have gladly been their cat!

A few years later when Jenson was acquired by Hal Leonard, I got that wish. It's been a great ride, gentlemen. Thank you for bringing me along. Meow!

SIDEBAR: Mac is one of the most creative choral arrangers I have ever known and once he shared a tidbit with me about his process: Somewhere in the piece he tries to have a "Mac Moment." It can be a key change, a chord progression, a rhythmic element or counter-melody that catches the singer and the listener off guard but in a good way. He's simply a genius!

John Jacobson
"It's Curtains for You!"

Yes, the rumors are true: I have slept with John…in a shared dorm room, Milikin University, 1982. Let me be clear, John Jacobson is perhaps the most creative and talented individual I have ever had the pleasure of collaborating with. When people ask what aspect of my career has been the most fun, this is my answer: Writing musicals with John is magic. Fast and furious. You should hear the adult outtakes!!

I digress…back to the sleeping thing! It was a brand-new dorm with aggressive air conditioning. Only a sheet was provided so in McGyver fashion, he grabbed the curtain (hooks and all) from his window for his bed and I followed suit for mine! Two fatigued clinicians finally got a good night's sleep. Avoiding those sharp hooks took some doing, however. Thanks, John, for 40 years of fun and creativity!

SIDEBAR: I've known John for 40 years and he is the "real deal." If you've ever heard him give a keynote, you understand what I mean. His dedication to music education and making people's lives better through music is legendary. His America Sings Foundation has donated thousands of dollars to feeding homeless children and bringing awareness to their plight. In addition, no one finds a better way to pay a compliment to a choir. I love his slogan…"It wasn't perfect but it WAS perfectly sincere!" I have used it many times myself and for my money, sincerity trumps accuracy. Thanks, John!

Greg Jasperse
Scat!

Please, don't go! Scat, get it? I think my first encounter with Greg was after being blown away by his "Voicedance" wordless choral. It's challenging, but if you're not familiar with it, give a listen. So, of course, I hold him in high esteem. Once we became friends, I invited him to our Summer Jazz and Show Choir Camp at College of the Siskiyous. Let me just say this…nobody makes a better or more lethal sidecar–not to mention his award-winning guacamole! Music, drink and food?? Yep…I think it goes with the territory.

I've learned a couple of cool things from him along the way. When teaching vocal improvisation or a written-out scat solo, de-emphasize the consonants. Use only enough to propel the line, much as an instrumentalist legato tongues a line. Students think they need to sing each syllable bah doo bah dwee, etc. However, the line needs to be legato (unless otherwise marked) with just a hint of b,d,b,d. I hope that makes sense.

The other somewhat sophisticated technique I learned is to add a breath accent to the release of the phrase. "Yeah" would be sung "yeah ah" with the "ah" added at the release. It's pretty cool. I expect after this book is released, I will be demonstrating the concept everywhere I go…but it will be well worth it.

"Never let pride stand in your way of making money."

Art Jenson - Grade unavailable

Art Jenson
"Taking a Chance on Me"

This is a long chapter, but I think it says a lot about doors opening and closing in my life.

In 1975, I was invited by my local music dealer to meet Bill Altice, the sales manager at Hal Leonard, as I was using the Hal Leonard Learning Unlimited series with my middle school band classes. Yes, I taught band along with choir…I loved it and, if truth be known, my bands were better than my choirs at the beginning of my career and I'm convinced it's because band has a method book and graded arrangements. Choir not so much so. But I digress.

Bill and I hit it off and he asked if I would become a Hal Leonard clinician for the band method. Of course, I said yes. I was 25 and eager to join the ranks of the published. Interestingly, I had written a guitar ensemble book with Jerry Snyder that was published two years earlier, so I had gotten a taste for royalties. Funny enough, I received a check for $500 for that book (a little less than my monthly take home), and never saw another dime. Just remember, there is value in the credential that publishing represents. I digress again!

So I became a known element at Hal Leonard by the then-vice-president, Art Jenson. He asked me to do a bit of guitar editing, which I did, and if you've read the Joyce Eilers chapter, you know that my choral pieces had been rejected by Hal Leonard a short time later.

But, as fate would have it, Art was let go and decided to start his own company, Jenson Publications. He needed a choral writer...yep, after having my pieces turned down at Hal Leonard, they were now the biggest-selling pieces of the year! "First, We Must Be Friends" and "Sinner Man" each sold upwards of 75,000 copies in 1977-78, and the rest is history. Even though Art was a bit of a bull in a China shop, I will be forever grateful that he believed in me and gave me the opportunity of a lifetime.

Alex Lacamoire
"Behind Every Great Songwriter"

His name may not be familiar to you, however, in the past few years, he has had a bigger impact on musical theater than anyone else. He orchestrated, and more than that, collaborated with both Lin-Manuel Miranda (*In The Heights, Hamilton,* etc.) and Pasek and Paul (*Dear Evan Hansen, The Greatest Showman,* etc.).

Just as George Martin was considered the 5th Beatle, I'm convinced that Alex has been critical to the success and musicality of the above-mentioned shows. How do I know that? Because he has to approve any arrangements done of tunes from those shows, arrangements created by me, Mac Huff, Mark Brymer and others.

Most importantly, his input has always been thoughtful, spot-on and it has offered improvement to all the arrangements that I have done. It has been a pleasure interfacing with someone who truly cares and understands what singers can and will do.

Gerry Lemieux
"Shout Inside"

The fact is a "choral master" can be anyone whom you learn an important technique from, and Gerry was one of those people. He taught in nearby Klamath Falls, Oregon. We are about the same age, so we sort of "grew up" together in the choral world. Many years ago, he was the adjudicator at our Northern Section CMEA (California) festival and I had my middle school choir perform that day.

Gerry said something to my students that codified how to get them to sing softly but with energy. It was a simple phrase with enormous impact:

"Shout inside"

It is a concept that is sometimes so hard to get across (particularly to younger singers), but they get this wonderful analogy and I use it often to bring choristers alive. Simply…"Shout inside!"

Thanks Gerry! You probably don't even know that you are a "choral master" to me and now, hopefully, others.

Ed Lojeski
"The Father of Pop Choral"

Early in my teaching career, Kirby Shaw had invited Ed to a gathering at his house after a local festival that he had judged, and I had the pleasure of attending as well.

A funny, prophetic phrase came out of him that I will never forget: "Someday some young person will take my career away." Little did I know that he was referring to me.

Now, I can't say that was ever my intention. In fact, my early works were 3-part mixed and aimed at middle school…an area that Ed did not focus on. As time went on, I, of course, branched out and eventually became his competitor at Jenson Publications. Little did he know that I adopted his method of lines that sing, playable piano parts and overall practicality.

Ed was a wonderful arranger and quite a character. He always wore the gold pendant that Elvis had given him (check out *Viva Las Vegas* and you'll see Ed playing piano) that said, "TCB," short for "Taking Care of Business."

In later years, when Ed would appear at a reading session, he would encourage attendees to "purchase those combo parts while you can," as they would go out of print. Digital has changed all of that, but if Ed were still alive, he'd probably still be encouraging folks to "purchase those combo parts!"

George Mattos
"Rush Up! Slow Down"

I had a very truncated choral music education. After my 6th grade experience with Ireta Cushing where I learned so much, I went on to junior high school where the vocal music offering was only "Girls Glee." Having specialized in getting young men to sing in middle school, I now understand the rationale…it's tough!

In high school, choir was just not a popular class, and although I was playing and singing in my rock band, I found my home in student government. So, when I began my college music education, I was playing "catch-up."

Fortunately, my community college director was amazing. Not only did he have love, passion and skill for choral music, but he was also an excellent sax player and had competed in the pole vault at the 1952 and 1956 Olympics…missing a medal by one position!

George was always bringing the latest music back from workshops and he was an early programmer of Scandinavian choral pieces such as "Aftonen" by Hugo Alfven. I loved the contemporary harmonies that have informed pieces like my "Rainstorm." The concept that sticks with me, however, is the idea of "rushing up" the front side of the phrase and slightly "slowing down" the back side. These are very subtle accelerations, but they tend to move the phrase forward and shape it beautifully. Thank you, George! I am forever grateful to have had you as a mentor.

Cristi Miller
"Oklahoooma!"

If you don't know Cristi, you should. So real and so much fun! The first time I met this Oklahoma writer, I thought, OKLAHOMA! All she needed was boots and a lasso (not Ted, the would-be soccer coach) and she would have been complete. A true force of nature, a consummate educator and spot-on writer. I have had the joy of seeing her grow, become Oklahoma ACDA President, instrumental in EEMC and best of all, lifelong friend. She reminds me that we are all still learning and growing and that we all start off a bit rough around the edges. In addition, she and I share the same "blue" sense of humor to which I heartily say, "Yee Haw!"

Larry Morton
"You ARE Hal Leonard Choral"

Larry Morton is probably not a name you are familiar with, however, he has a major impact on the music that you program, as he is the CEO of Hal Leonard LLC, my publishing company. He and I landed at Hal Leonard at about the same time. He came over from the Roland Corporation, has a degree in music from North Texas and is a genuinely nice guy. He also has been instrumental in the growth of the company and is responsible for creating a worldwide publishing force of nature.

Several years ago, while I was visiting the company's headquarters in Milwaukee, he invited me to lunch. I was quite flattered and jumped at the chance to spend a little one-on-one time with him. It's amazing what one lunch can do to validate 30-plus years of teaching, composing and arranging. At one point in time he said, "Roger, you and John (Jacobson) ARE Hal Leonard Choral." Wow! Wow! Perhaps the *face* of choral might have been more appropriate, but I'm not one to argue! He and I have not always agreed, however, we both have this amazing company's best interests at heart.

You may be interested to know that education, i.e., band and choir music, only makeup about 10 percent of the revenue for the company, the remainder being guitar, piano, vocal and other "mass market" or "rack books" as they are called. I am always appreciative that "choral," at about 5 percent, gets as much attention as it does.

Another little-known fact is that Hal Leonard was founded by two brothers, Harold "Hal" and Everett "Leonard" Edstrom and their friend Roger Busdicker in the early 1950s. The two brothers were band directors who would routinely travel to New York to license music for their bands and, ultimately, publish it. In later years, CEO Keith Mardak would use the additional 10 percent that the company would gain from instrumental/choral sales to outbid other print publishing entities when seeking rights to a catalog (i.e., Disney, Sony, etc.). And as Paul Harvey would say, "Now you know the rest of the story."

Louis (Lou) Morell
"The Joy of Teaching"

Lou Morell was my first guitar teacher. I took lessons from him from the time I was 10 until about 14. He was an amazing player and teacher and he would, on occasion, have to cancel a lesson to fly to Vegas to accompany various stars. Little did I know, he was a member of The Wrecking Crew who played on most of the recordings of the late '60s and '70s, including The Beach Boys, The Mamas and the Papas, The Association and more.

When I was 18, my brother Richard's singing group, The Match, were recording one of my songs and…guess who was the guitarist on the session? None other than Lou Morell. I remember standing in the booth and him looking up at me with a big smile on his face. It was at that moment I learned the joy of teaching and the joy of seeing your students go on to do great things. Although my song never made the album, I wouldn't trade that moment of revelation for the world. I often tell my college students, "If you decide to be a music educator, you WILL get tired. You WILL get frustrated, but you WILL NEVER feel like your life did not matter!" Here's to teachers and students.

Teddy Neely
"I Don't Care What You Do!"

As I mentioned earlier, at 18, I started doing some studio work as an electric bass player in Los Angeles, for which I was somewhat ill-prepared. I had good ears, read chord symbols, played well, but did not read very well.

As I walked into the studio I remember listening to this great playback of a tune that would become a #1 hit for Sly and the Family Stone…"Dance to the Music." I remember thinking…"What a great groove."

As I sat down and got my bass out and connected to the amp, the producer put down a piece of music with lots of notes on it. I turned to Teddy—who, by the way, had achieved stardom as Jesus in the movie *Jesus Christ, Superstar*—and said, "Do you want it exactly as written?" His response was priceless:

"I don't care if you fart in the mic as long as it sounds good!" There you have it…a lesson for us all…but don't try it!

As I'm writing this, I am reminded, however, of a rather unusual "sound" that we used when recording "Ewok Celebration." Alan Billingsley and I were trying to create background animal sounds to emulate the *Star Wars* bar scene. We were recording at Wayne Cook's studio, which was located in his back yard. Wayne's claim to fame was as a keyboardist and songwriter with the group Player, which had the hit "Baby Come Back."

That was how he financed his own studio. Wayne had a little pug dog who liked to snort so…you guessed it…if you can find a copy, you'll hear dog snorts mixed into the sound effects during the introduction.

Which reminds me of yet another crazy moment. During the recording of my first musical *TEEN* in Chicago, someone had shared the rather racy joke: *"What did the elephant say to the naked man? How do you eat with that thing?"* Sure enough, during an interlude where we needed "chatter," one of the studio singers utters…"How do you eat with that thing?" If you can find the old vinyl, it is yours for the listening!   ☺

The New York Voices
"The Most Musical Moment"

About 15 years ago, after admiring Darmon Meader, Kim Nazarian, Lauren Kinhan and Peter Eldridge's work for years, I ventured 250 miles south to Oakland, California, to hear them live at Yoshi's, the famous jazz club.

Now I've heard a lot of performances in my day, including Barbra Streisand's Hollywood Bowl premier, The Doors, also at the Bowl, James Taylor, Amy Grant, Al Jarreau, Dizzy Gillespie and many more, but none matches the total impact that NYV had on me that night.

I suppose one can say that a lot depends on your receptive state when it comes to the impact of art, whether it be live performance, a movie, a book, visual art or other. But on this night, I witnessed the ultimate in musicianship. From stellar and creative arrangements to flawless and effortless (appearing) performances…it just doesn't get any better IMHO. I had to mention these folks, as we have since become friends and my admiration grows each time we interface. Stellar musicians and people…the best kind! Their performance remains the most musical moment of my life.

SIDEBAR: As a bit of a sidebar, at intermission they sat at a table and sold CDs, which at the time I thought was unusual; however, I have come to find out that vocal jazz is a very small piece of the music market, particularly in the United States. Europe has a much larger interest and market for this niche style of music, but then again Europe has an affinity for other niche things like health care, social programs and the like. Oops…I'm giving away my political position! In reality, I'm a moderate and have voted across the aisle, but in my heart, I believe that the United States has the resources to provide a better life for its citizens, if only we had the political will. I am hopeful that the younger generation gets this and will ultimately make our country better. It is my hope and prayer.

Kirby Shaw
"You Can Do This!"

I often say that I would be playing and singing in your neighborhood Holiday Inn if it weren't for Kirby Shaw.

Even though I've been creating and performing music on a regular basis since childhood, I never considered myself "music major" material. After a year at Whittier College taking general education classes, I moved with a few high school friends to Northern California. If you think San Francisco is Northern California, you'd be wrong! There is another 350 miles of state above and I ended up at this small community college (College of the Siskiyous) in Weed, California. The town of Weed, named after its founder, Abner Weed (not the plant), sits just 60 miles from the Oregon border.

Who in their right mind would leave Los Angeles, the hotbed of commercial music, and venture to this small town to further his/her music career? ME! It was a fluke, quite frankly, or simply meant to be. I decided to take a few music classes, i.e., theory, musicianship etc., and you probably can guess who the instructor was… the unpublished Kirby Shaw. Let me just say, I finally had found my home. I loved learning to read music better, understand why chords moved and related the way they did and general rehearsal practice from this amazing teacher.

Shortly after my arrival, Kirby instituted his first vocal jazz ensemble. It was called Vocal/Instrumental Ensemble, as he also wrote for rhythm section and four horns. I played guitar and sang for him and every day was like manna from heaven. He would pass out a new arrangement at each rehearsal in his impeccable pencil manuscript. It was there that I knew I wanted to be a teacher. But in our small schools, one would often have to teach instrumental music as well as vocal. I distinctly remember asking him..."Kirby, how will I teach clarinet?" He answered..."You'll get a clarinet, a book and stay a week ahead of the kids! You CAN DO THIS!" Although I had taken instrumental methods classes as part of my undergraduate work, I knew he was right...I spent the summer practicing clarinet, flute, saxophone, trumpet and trombone...the beginning band instruments.

Interesting thing...my bands were better than my choirs!! Even though I was an applied vocal major, I was in no way prepared to teach middle school choir. The other advantage that instrumental music had was a method book and graded arrangements. Vocal music was more of a free for all. It was during this time that I had an epiphany..."You call yourself a songwriter... write your 7th and 8th graders a song!" I did just that and fashioned it after the 3-part mixed formula pioneered by Joyce Eilers. The rest is history. "First, We Must Be Friends" and "Sinner Man" became hits for me and, more importantly, successful vehicles for fostering singing in kids, which has always been my driving force. Thanks Kirby, for believing in me and for always saying..."You Can Do This!"

SIDEBAR: Kirby was a stickler for accuracy in all things...just look at his scores...every measure numbered, vocal inflections, etc. I too believe we should all at least start with the correct notes, and I often use this phrase with my students regarding the parts of a song they don't know very well..."No one knows better than you where you are faking it!" Just let me know...we can fix it if you tell me; otherwise the piece is never as good as it can be.

SIDEBAR #2: Kirby would often say when it comes to vocal improvisation..."You're only a half-step away from something that works!" I'll take that one step further by saying...it works everywhere! ☺

Audrey Snyder
"Grateful"

I loved Audrey's first publication "Guitar Man" and used it frequently when teaching in the '80s. She is a gifted writer with many wonderful pieces, but, more importantly, she is a gifted friend. Like Emily Crocker, she is a quiet force of nature and a spot-on editor of the "Discovery" series at Hal Leonard. When I submit a piece, she will, on occasion, make a suggestion and I will say to myself, "Why didn't I think of that!?!" But the most important thing she did for me was to gift a book called *A Grateful Heart* by M. J. Ryan. Simple, short, daily offerings on the importance of being grateful. It set me on a course that has brought much peace and joy to my life. I am grateful for you, Audrey, and so much more.

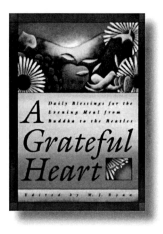

Andy Waterman
"WISMOC"

In the early '80s, Andy Waterman became the go-to producer/engineer for educational recordings, including many of my choral tracks, those for *Music Express Magazine* and McGraw Hill textbooks as well as major film and popular recordings. Not only does he have great "ears," but he understands the sound needed for education. Our budgets in educational recording are one-tenth that of commercial budgets; whereas a pop record might cost $10,000, ours would be $1,000.

They must be done quickly by first-call studio players and singers in about an hour each. Whenever we wanted to "do it over" after a small glitch, we would turn to each other and say, "Will it sell more copies?" Usually not, so we created a shortcut by merely uttering *WISMOC*. True story. Thanks, Andy, for your years of extra, free hours making things better for directors and their singers.

Jack Zaino
"One Child Born"

Zuckerburg, Zemeckis, Zellweger, Zaino… what did these people do in school while waiting for their name to be called anyway!?!? Get smart, I think :) Anyway, Jack is a new friend whom I met in 2019 at the Connecticut ACDA Fall Conference (thanks, Amanda Hanzlik, for the invite!). I was a presenter and their keynote speaker. Anytime I am at a conference, I make an effort to attend other sessions because I love learning. This particular one was "Contemporary A Cappella Arranging" hosted by Shams Ahmed, who is associated with Pentatonix and I didn't want to miss it. I entered the room late and found a seat by the wall near the door. I glanced to the back of the room and saw a young teacher and thought…I'm so glad that I see more and more young teachers entering the profession!

At the end of the session Jack rushed up to me and said, "Will you sign this, please?" I was startled, as it was my first published piece, "First, We Must Be Friends." My response: "WHERE did you get this?" He simply said, "My school library." As usual, I wrote, what would become prophetic, "Jack…you're the best!"

A few days after the conference I got his FB request. I discovered he too was an arranger and had just published his first arrangement. By the printing of this book, I'm sure he will have over a dozen in print and many more to come.

The amazing thing is that his writing is invariably similar to mine: straightforward, accurate and singable. He's a teacher and a singer and I believe it shows in his writing. I've also learned that much as I sought out Joyce Eilers by driving 650 miles to Seattle to a workshop, he sought out Emily Crocker and drove 650 miles to Columbus, Ohio, for a Joy of Singing. It seems to have paid off.

We have since collaborated on a piece or two and continue to set a high bar for each other. Collaboration and a bit of competition is a good thing. It is only fitting that this book finish with his chapter, as he is the heir apparent and I am so glad. In the immortal words of Billie Holiday (and David Clayton Thomas), *"There'll be one child born in this world to carry on."* I, or we, can all rest easy. Popular choral music is in good hands.

Epilogue
"Family"

I wouldn't be where I am today without the support and encouragement of my amazing family.

MOM. Ruthevelyn Smith Emerson. The unconditional lover. Brilliant musician and supporter of my music. Her wise words have become my mantra: The three things one needs to be happy are something to do, someone to love, and something to hope for. I am fortunate to have all three…blessed beyond measure.

Years ago, when I was transporting her to radiation treatments, I asked her, "What did you want for your three sons? (Our dad had passed when I was two, and my brothers eight and ten, and she set the example of a strong and capable single parent.) She gave me a tremendous respect for women in general as well. I thought she'd say, "Nice homes, good jobs, solid marriages etc.," What she said to me seemed simple yet far-reaching…"To love and be loved." It sums it all up and it is my wish for all who read this book.

My brother, Richard Derwingson, (we have different last names as my step-father adopted me, but my older brothers had left for college and didn't desire a name change…man, am I glad, Emerson is so much easier to remember and spell!) for his continuing encouragement and support. Richard and I collaborated on the *TEEN* series of musicals and he has written and recorded countless pieces. He is a much better musician, quite frankly, but never reminds me!

My loving wife, Mari. It sounds like Mary but was originally Mariellen, hence the spelling. She's a wonderful musician and lyric soprano who taught my 5th and 6th graders to sing like a select children's chorus, which made 7th and 8th grade choir a breeze—not to mention a very grateful high school choir director to have such a fine feeder program. She puts up with me "not being there" even when I'm home but engaged in creating. Thanks, honey. I love you!

Son, Ryder...born Cassandra, for an amazing journey and growth. If you haven't performed his "Wayfaring Stranger" (Cassandra Emerson, Hal Leonard), you should. He is a fine musician, has better ears than me, and continues to act and sing in regional theater to our delight. When people say we are such great parents for supporting his transition, I say, it's simple. You want your child to be comfortable in their own skin. When it comes to courage, it is all his, not ours. For anyone in a similar setting, we did some family counseling early on and the toughest part is that you feel like Cassandra (Cassie) has died. The counselor made that go away in one simple phrase..."Just remember, it was Ryder all along." Done. Love you, man.

Finally, our youngest, Kayla. She has my outgoing personality and her mom's athletic prowess. Never a dull moment. Often pitching me songs..."You should arrange this one, Dad." A fine musician in her own right, but at 29, she's making more money than me in the tech world! She keeps me on my toes and can fix my computer problems. I love you, sweetie, too.

One last...my step-father, Jim. Thanks for carrying on family traditions, for unconditional love and giving me a great last name. At 88, you're still sharp as a tack! I wish I had your genes!!! Love you.

To all who have made it this far and those who haven't, thanks for indulging me, for singing my songs, and making my life grand. I am forever grateful.

– RE

"I've learned that people will forget what you said, people will forget what you did, but people will never forget how you made them feel."
... Maya Angelou

Appendix 1 - Jeffreyisms

51 IDEAS TO ENGAGE OUR SINGERS
(and avoid routine)
Dr. Jeffrey Benson – San Jose State University

1. Do a warm-up in the middle of rehearsal

2. Pull out a piece from earlier in the year, just to sing through it once and put it away

3. Switch the order of the solfege syllables in your warm-up

4. Sing a sight-singing exercise or musical phrase backwards

5. Sightread at the end of rehearsal

6. Ask your singers to write a haiku about the piece (or about the text)

7. User Dalcroze to walk to a fabulous recording you want to share

8. Have your singers create a meme about one of your pieces

9. Ask your singers to write a new or companion text for the piece

10. Change the orientation of the room or alter the seating arrangement in some way

11. Bring a prop to class that relates to one of the songs and don't mention it until partway through rehearsal

12. Have them conduct along with you

13. Ask individuals to take turns conducting the choir

14. Have singers interlock arms while singing

15. Have a small group of students sit out and listen, take notes and provide feedback

16. Only students in certain birthday months sing phrases

17. Ask students to lead sectionals or mini-rehearsals on student-led songs

18. Use Laban gestures (e.g. dab, flick, float, glide) with singers to teach articulation

19. Have students text each other the answer to a question you've asked

20. Step to the rhythm of the text

21. Have students stand in circles by section

22. Sing in the cafeteria or gym (rehearse a mini performance at lunch)

23. Sing with the lights off

24. Sing the piece twice as fast or twice as slow as usual

25. Step to the tactus

26. Try to avoid predictable half-step changes for each warm-up; bounce around keys or warm-up by whole step

27. Shape phrases with "choir gang signs"

28. Choose a rehearsal where you do not speak at all with your choir (everything is mimed)

29. Step to the subdivision (micro beat)

30. Have students text each other an interpretation of poetry, then share anonymously

31. Sing in a full circle around the room

32. Have students stand in mixed quartets

33. Have students act out the story of the text

34. Play solfege games where you add motions to several (or all) of the scale degrees (e.g. snap your fingers on "fa" or stomp your feet on "re")

35. Ask singers to hold a chair while they're singing in order to engage core

36. Sing in the stairwell (or another extremely resonant space in the building)

37. Have sections leave out a measure of music (audiate) as they rehearse

38. Rehearse outside

39. Have students create a skit about certain pieces

40. Ask the students to hold hands while singing

41. Have singers record themselves on a device while singing with the full ensemble

42. Have singers send each other those recordings and provide feedback for a colleague

43. Alternate phrases of a song, so each row of the choir only sings a phrase at a time

44. After learning the foreign language fully, sing the terrible English version underneath

45. Stand and sing to the row behind

46. Have students sing with a chair in their arms, out in front of their bodies

47. Singers can compose a new fugue theme or melody to complement the repertoire

48. Have students switch parts in the middle of a piece (sightread a new section's part)

49. Include trivia in the rehearsals (related to the poetry, music history, theory, etc.)

50. Have small groups create a skit/commercial for your concert or to sell the piece/poetry

51. Sing solfege scales and leave out a different note each day

Appendix 2 - Rogerisms

Roger Emerson is a professional composer and arranger with over 1,000 choral titles in print and over 30 million copies in circulation. He is the most widely performed composer/ arranger of popular choral music and vocal jazz in the world today. His works include the choral arrangements of Josh Groban's You Raise Me Up, Season's of Love, from RENT, Defying Gravity from WICKED, Joyful, Joyful from SISTER ACT, Don't Stop Believin' from GLEE, and most recently, My Shot from HAMILTON. In addition, his vocal jazz arrangements of Over The Rainbow, Vincent, Blue Skies and I Wish are some of the most performed of all-time. Mr. Emerson has been the recipient of ASCAP's Standard Award for 30 years running and his works have been performed at the White House, Carnegie Hall and the Kennedy Center. He is in constant demand as a lecturer on pop music, vocal jazz and the changing voice and has appeared at numerous MENC, ACDA and JEN conferences.

Check out these websites:
www.rogeremerson.com & www.sing678.com